A Grand Design
The Art of the Victoria and Albert Museum
INTERIORES
Rugs&Carpets
Oriental

# BRIGER+BRIGER

PYRAMIDES DE MEMPHIS

# BRIGER+BRIGER

## Comfortable & Joyous Homes

CITY, COUNTRY, AND LAKESIDE

Cris and Paul Briger
Photography by Michel Zabé

RIZZOLI
NEW YORK

First published in the United States of America in 2007
by Rizzoli International Publications, Inc.
300 Park Avenue South
New York, New York 10010
www.rizzoliusa.com



2008 2009 2010 / 10 9 8 7 6 5 4 3 2

Printed in China

ISBN-10: 0-8478-2999-5
ISBN-13: 978-0-8478-2999-6

Library of Congress Control Number: 2001012345

Project Editor: Sandra Gilbert
Art Direction: Carmen Cordera Lascurain
Design and prepress: Emilio Breton
Drafft Diseñadores Asociados, México

Cris and Paul Briger are the principals of Briger + Briger, an American design firm specializing in interior design, architecture, and landscaping.

www.brigerbriger-design.com

Front matter photography page 2 Lakeside House, bedroom hall; page 4 Country House, living room; page 7 City House, entrance; page 8 City House, living room; page 10 Country House, front hall; page 15 Country House, dining room; pages 16–17 Country House, terrace.
Back matter photography page 240 Country House, terrace.

Viva México!

PALAZZO CENCI
PALAZZO GIUSTINIANI

# CONTENTS

With few exceptions, people seek comfortable places in which to live. Even at eighteenth-century Versailles, the French royal family would desert the grand and glorious public rooms (including their official bedrooms) to move into what even by our standards are tiny, ill-lit rooms—albeit beautiful, warm, and cozy, facing on dim courtyards, for amusements and sleep—returning to chilly grandeur only in the morning. The image of Louis XIV dining with his morganatic wife, Madame de Maintenon, in front of a fire in the small salon of her diminutive apartment at the palace has always struck me as so surprisingly bourgeois, yet perhaps the only identifiably human activity in his life.

Comfort is an overused word but what it really signifies is very important. It is not simply good upholstery, high-thread-count sheets, superb mattresses, and well-placed lighting. Basically, comfort can be judged by how well an environment suits its purpose—in other words, how a house meets its obligation to bring ease of living to its occupants. After meeting such basics as shelter from the elements, security, and plumbing, comfort is, among other things, how a house sits in its landscape with ease of access to entry doors when the weather is inclement; the placement and flow of rooms so as to insure privacy and convenience; adequate and well-lit storage facilities for dishware, clothing, and luggage; and the location of electric sockets close to where they are needed. It also extends to the relationship of the proprietor and family to their guests and others. On a very elementary level, one of the most surprising absences in many well-designed houses is good bathroom lighting. Down lights over mirrors provide dramatic effect but, without adequate general lighting, produce disagreeable distortions and hamper grooming. Similarly, electric sockets for hairdryers are hardly ever placed near mirrors in bathrooms or in bedrooms.

After comfort in the broadest sense is identified and provided, what remains is to create beautiful or simply handsome spaces that fill the eye with joy and reflect the personality and aspirations of the occupants. A designer seeks to create, rescue, revive, or redo the very contents of their clients' lives, to fulfill the purpose of a house and express the personality of its occupants. This task is easier when the client has passions for fine art, *objets d'art*, or furniture. But the absence of an interest in the decorative arts is no barrier to creating a joyous residence. It does require that the designer ascertain what it is the client really wants to live with and reflect that in his domain—in other words, including such personal items as photographs and books, as well as certain colors and textures. This is very rewarding as it often becomes clear that the client has hitherto unrecognized affinities.

Much of current interior design falls into the trap of creating houses that are too bare, too safe, too impersonal, too flatly grand, and all seemingly haunted by the fear of making a mistake or being criticized by a peer. While a designer can't or shouldn't force an unwilling round peg into a square hole, it is possible to devise houses for living without creating the impersonality of a hotel.

A major part of the real comfort and joy of living in a residence arises from the degree to which it reflects the occupants. This is the personality of a house. Houses don't necessarily gain personality by the quality or quantity of their contents. Even great and grand houses needn't be populated entirely by equally great and grand pieces. While great contemporary or antique pieces are certainly desirable to give substance to a room, amusing and charming ones add enormously to deflate pomposity and establish the character of the occupants. The extraordinary French designer, the late Madeleine Castaing, remarked that every room requires some "bad taste." I have always taken that statement not to mean that a room requires something ugly or vulgar, but simply the need for something that is out of character in the context of what predominates in the room—something that indicates a strong personal affection of the proprietor, who chooses to place it despite its apparent incongruity.

If an excellent and costly piece of furniture or fine art is not immediately affordable or locatable, it is useful to purchase something inexpensive of the right style and scale and wait for the opportunity to buy the good piece. If properly selected, that inexpensive piece often becomes an object of desire and, while it might not remain in its original prime location, it can be moved and enjoyed elsewhere in a home.

A residence needn't and shouldn't remain fixed for a lifetime. People change over time and their tastes change. To achieve the desired degree of change doesn't necessarily mean that a residence be entirely renovated. It is surprising how much a new wall color, a new fabric, a new piece of furniture, or merely the rearrangement of existing furniture will do to change the personality of a room or a house.

Houses should be as organic as gardens. While it may sometimes seem sad that interiors are the least permanent of the decorative arts, houses that remain forever intact frequently acquire the aspect of a museum, no longer expressing the current tastes or interests of their occupants. It is interesting to look at books of residences decorated in earlier decades. While one can appreciate the skill of the decoration, the overall style is rarely anything that one would want to replicate, except for particular elements, and even those need a new perspective to make them work.

In recent years, many new houses have been constructed in the United States, rivaling in size those built in the last two decades of the nineteenth century. However, large houses and abundant possessions require very substantial maintenance if they are to be enjoyed and not become an impediment to living. The idea of having twelve guest rooms where the lady—or gentleman—of the house has to make the beds and vacuum the carpets becomes a real deterrent to filling those rooms, even with the best of friends. Better to have friends stay in small numbers or in a local hotel, than resent their presence while changing the sheets.

Understanding what it takes to run a large house and maintain properly a collection of fine and decorative arts is an aspect of providing for the comfort of living. This also applies to the size of the property and how that property is developed into manageable spaces in the absence of a nineteenth-century-size staff of gardeners. Beautiful, endless lawns are a joy to look at but not when they are improperly cut or full of crabgrass. Merely to be able to afford sufficient service for care and tending both inside and outside residences doesn't fulfill that need. That's not to say one shouldn't turn down the opportunity to buy a château or build its equivalent, but it is important to be aware of how difficult it is to keep one up, even from a non-economic standpoint.

This book presents an in-depth photographic study of three houses that have been built or remodeled and decorated by our firm. The approaches taken to develop the houses and their gardens reflect the demands and interests of their residents as well as the environments in which the houses are situated. The houses differ widely from one another: the first, a spacious and sophisticated urban dwelling; the second, a large and formal country house; and, the third, a sprawling and casual lakeside weekend retreat. The function of each house is different, which is reflected in its decoration. However, all three have in common the quality of deep comfort and that they are all visually interesting and stimulating. Within each interior, the artwork, furniture, carpets, and fabrics express the function of the houses and the interests and passions of the occupants. In addition, all of the houses have in common a sense of orderliness and balance, the latter achieved either by symmetry in numbers or symmetry in the visual weight of objects, colors, or fabrics. Even the largest of the houses—the country house—eschews grandiosity and has intimate spaces that permit small groups not to feel overwhelmed by the overall size of the house. The ceilings while high—12 feet—are not too high to preclude a sense of coziness. I recall once having cocktails in the grand salon of the Circlo de Caccia Club in Rome and thinking that there really was no ceiling to the room—it being so high, and wondering what it was like to be there when it was the grand salon of the Borghese palace. But then, of course, the immensity of the room was meant chiefly to impress upon visitors the enormous wealth and power of the prince's family and not for comfort or mere enjoyment of his family. And, like the French royal family at Versailles, the Borgheses did retreat to small rooms when simply living and not needing to impose their grandeur upon fledgling rivals. While I am not being puritanical about the desire to impress, one should at least be aware in building or buying a large house that impressionable spaces are generally not livable spaces and one needs intimate spaces (as did the various "Louis" et al.) for ordinary pursuits and comforts.

Finally, those interested in houses and gardens are frequently disappointed that many books or magazines on residences show generally only a few parts of the house, typically the reception rooms, a bedroom or two, and occasionally a kitchen. There is no such disappointment here. The houses are shown nearly in their entirety, with the exception of the service rooms, to give a real sense of how the house designs work as a whole.

CÔTES

# City house

## A SPACIOUS URBAN DWELLING

The idea of a "house in the city" instantly conjures up a sense of duty and responsibility, for the city is generally the place where one conducts business affairs, educates children, and participates in civic and charitable activities. A city house should therefore serve as a haven to revitalize the flagging spirit of its occupants as they return from burdensome obligations, running errands, and battling traffic.

The house portrayed here is a spacious dwelling surrounded on all sides by a compact garden and overlooking one of the city's green areas. It was built in the 1940s and, by the standards of Mexico City where the house is located, is often considered "too old" to provide appropriate living quarters. While a place of enormous contrasts and conflicts, Mexico City still manages to offer both natural and man-made beauty and has all the qualities of joy, sophistication, and gaiety that probably can still only be found in a Latin American capital.

When purchased, the house had excellent "bones" and a very rational flow of well-proportioned spaces, surprisingly reminiscent of a large, pre-war New York apartment, even to the extent of having uniformly high ceilings throughout and plaster beams and moldings. The principal rooms are all on one level, with a partial lower floor where the main entrance, office, service rooms, and storage are located. Aside from completely new decoration, the house required new floors, total renovation of the baths and kitchen, an overall rethinking of indoor spaces to bring more natural light into the interior, as well as the sprucing up of outdoor areas. The property also contained a cottage in the garden, which, at the time it was purchased, comprised a rabbit warren of very small rooms, one of which charmingly housed a Buddhist shrine. This structure was renovated into two sizable guest rooms with a shared bath.

We have done the house informally and furnished it with a mélange of furniture styles and art to divert and please the eye of its occupants. New windows and internal and external doors were added to bring more light into the house and provide a visual enlargement to the rooms. To promote further a sense of spaciousness, all of the rooms were painted in an oyster white color: the only exception to this color scheme in the main house is found in the breakfast room, which has been painted with wide horizontal stripes to give width to a narrow space. In several rooms, narrow shelves were installed along the walls to support the owners' burgeoning and ever-changing collection of paintings, thus avoiding the need to replaster nail holes as frequent changes are made.

The house hides behind high ivy-clad walls that serve as pleasing frames to the property from within and without the house. The house is truly a private stage for the lives of its inhabitants and the guests who enter it.

ST. AUBIN

## VESTIBULE

The vestibule of the house on the ground floor gives a foretaste of the eclecticism of the house's decoration: a framed Japanese needlepoint of a tiger's head hangs above a French *tôle peintre* grape basket now used to hold umbrellas; a grained and eglomisé early-nineteenth-century Italian mirror is mounted above an eighteenth-century Mexican Chippendale console table (which looks as if it could walk on its own). An important function of an interior designer is to provide an attractive and congenial display of what the client likes or possesses, even when those elements have no visible cultural or aesthetic relationship. The designer should take what is important to the client and strive to make a pleasing tableau, which often requires a great deal of trial and error.

## MAIN HALL

The principal rooms of this house are located on one level. From the vestibule, a twisting stairway climbs to the main hall. A main hall is not simply a passageway, but is an important space where one receives guests, and therefore should strongly set the tone for the rest of the house. Here, one immediately encounters Catherine Warren's powerful triptych variation on Hokusai's *Great Wave*, which gives vitality to the French daybed beneath it. The daybed is covered in Pierre Frey's "Petit Parc" fabric that appears to be antique and gives credibility to the age of the piece, which may or may not be eighteenth century.

At the entrance of the bedroom hall off the main hall, there is a large nineteenth-century needlepoint version of Rembrandt Peale's portrait of George Washington that was found in a Mexico City antiques market; this work adds impact without crowding the main hall's already amply used wall spaces. A pair of nickel-plated column lamps rests on a late-eighteenth-century console table; their light is beautifully reflected in two long, rectangular mirrors.

The metal screen is engraved with passages from the nineteenth-century *Book of Manners* by M. Carreño, relating to proper dress at social events: one paragraph directs ladies to leave their shoulders and arms bare and wear abundant and bright jewels at grand balls and the opera. The screen was discovered at a modern furniture show and amuses guests whose families were brought up to follow the dictates of Sr. Carreño. The monochromatic screen allows the wall against which it sits to become a significant way station for the eye, without having another painting or adding more color to an already colorful space. The perfect "pet dog" in front of the screen is an early-twentieth-century American candy box made of papier-mâché; a Victorian-period dwarf chaise longue is sometimes placed next to it. The Ingo Maurer chandelier creates a distinctly modern "umbrella" over the space; its dangling notepapers have been supplemented with private family messages.

Del Traje en General

The main hall leads into the living and dining rooms through heavy Romanesque-type archways that are a common feature in houses by the same architect/engineer Jorge Del Rio. The small rondel from the first decade of the twentieth century is made of papier-mâché and celebrates the "brilliance" of the thirty-year rule of Porfirio Diaz, which led directly to the Mexican Revolution in 1910. The curving stairway rises from the vestibule on the ground floor and the principal entrance of the house. The niche on the stairwell was electrically wired and covered with opaque glass as a means of making this "dated" feature more acceptable to the owners, in order to avoid eliminating an original architectural element. It also adds light to the stairwell.

A Grand Design
LARRY RIVERS
BOSPHORUS
PARIS

## LIVING ROOM

Here, the fireplace has not been made the focal point of the living room's furniture. While attractive, having the principal pieces arranged around a hearth can be limiting to a room's function, unless it is large enough to allow other furniture groupings. The mirror frames above the chimneypiece are made of red painted carton and resemble Baroque-period frames covered in fabric with metal stubs. They complement a photograph of Neo-classical statues from Deborah Turbeville's book *Unseen Versailles*. These items add historic references of the Baroque to the room without using actual pieces from that period, which would have had a more ponderous presence than was desired. To one side of the fireplace, a black and gold Napoleon III side chair serves as a side table. It still retains the burlap underlining with which it was found—and probably always will. The Chinese-style blue-and-white plate on the chimneypiece was made in Mexico during the eighteenth century, when Chinese porcelain arrived at the port of Acapulco; as these porcelains spread throughout the country, they inspired local potters to simulate the Chinese patterns. The gilt metal dog dating from the 1940s in front of the chimneypiece is a mystery as to its origins and purpose, if other than simply decorative. The chimneypiece itself, in Neo-classical style, is original to the house, but a seven-inch-high additional shelf on top as well as extra width gave it a heaviness that competed with the delicate Neo-classical elements; it was therefore modified by reducing its height and width. The arched doorway to the left of the fireplace was opened up to allow more light and reduce the sense of the room's rectilinear stiffness.

In order to control the colors and patterns in the living room, nearly all of the books have been covered in brown craft paper and given title and author labels. The books that had lost their covers are also protected. A similar effect, of course, could have been achieved by filling the bookcase with beautiful leather–bound volumes, but at much greater cost and certainly without whimsy.

The use of the same colorful toile on the upholstered pieces ties together the diverse types of seating as well as the room itself. The curtain fabric, a cotton duck onto which pinked silk "tails" were sewn, was custom-made when it was found that the fabric had been discontinued. The modern white and gray lacquer bookcase serves the practical purpose of shelving books and, in its closed cupboards on either side, storing any "odds and ends" that don't need to be in full sight. It also cuts through the overall traditional furnishing of the room with a functional and contemporary splash that prevents the entire space from being too "traditional." The small turquoise-and-white table with similarly colored tile is eighteenth-century Ottoman, and was discovered at a flea market.

Among the decorative objects in the bookcase, this pretty "mask" vase was one of a pair of fine eighteenth-century Staffordshire pieces; sadly, its "mate" was lost in a previous household move. The crackled "wine bottle" with a "melting candle" on top, one of a pair, a caricaturistic feature of old-fashioned "Italian" restaurants, was made in Murano, Italy, in the 1950s. The small bowl is also one of a pair and is probably nineteenth-century Meissen. The small nineteenth-century chair covered in a black horsehair fabric was made for cigar smokers to draw up to a fireplace; its two round drawers for cigars on either end of the back roll are still redolent of tobaccos from another era. It is convenient to have a number of small chairs to accommodate more seating than could be afforded by regular-size chairs. The diminutive bookcase next to the chair—one of a rickety pair that does double duty as a side table—was purchased in Paris from the shop of the late Madeleine Castaing, who was an antiquarian as well as an interior decorator. She chose her customers even more carefully than her stock: mere willingness to purchase at the madame's incredibly high prices was only the first qualification for a buyer's suitability. She dearly loved her shop inventory as much as what she placed in her own houses and parted with a piece only after long and flirtatious bargaining, which might linger over several visits. However, the desired item never disappeared before the return visit.

ITALIAN PAINTING
LES EBENISTES DU XIX SIECLE
INTERIORES EN MEXICO
Provence Interiors
ALBERT HADLEY

The living room leads into a small library/television room, and the doorway has been left uncovered to allow a view of the greenery beyond the far window, creating a sense of not really being confined indoors. Of course, it also adds additional light into the room. The oriental runner guides the eye to the space beyond as well as adding interest to the living room floor which, like all rooms in the house (other than the kitchen), has been covered simply in polished, unstained oak strips. On the wall, a rustic Art Deco rondel found in the Marché aux Puces in Paris surmounts a high-style Consulate-period commode. Both were acquired long before this house was purchased, without any idea as to where they would be placed, but pieces that are loved always find a place. The clock on the console table is a particularly beautiful example of a genre that was popular in France after the revolution. It was originally located in the main hall of the house but has since found a new perch in the living room.

## LIBRARY

The library boasts four large windows that look out over a green zone of the city. It is furnished comfortably for reading, watching television, and also for enjoying amateur piano recitals. There are two types of readers: those who discard new books after reading them, and those who keep all their books to be reminded of the pleasure derived from them (and, more dangerously, to lend with the dubious hope of their return). The latter describes the owners, and an ever-growing collection of books usually enters the house here and, once read, goes on to fill the shelves of other rooms. On the wall, the painting of a laborer scything a field is an early-twentieth-century work by a Belgian artist and presents a wonderful "window" to a sunny world on a dull day. The Petit Jacob "sultan figure" is a perfume burner which here serves as a bookend. When the house was purchased, this room had a fireplace on the wall below the shelves displaying the watercolors. It was off-center and would have made the room impossible to furnish and use rationally, so it was eliminated.

The Children of Pride -2- THE EDGE OF THE SWORD
The Children of Pride -3- THE NIGHT SEASON
ANNA KOMNENE The Alexiad

A trio of porcelain "nodders" (figures in porcelain or wood with moving heads on metal prongs) provides a change of decorative medium from the watercolors on the shelves above the television set. A pair of Chinese figures bearing candleholders on top of the dresser is from western China, close to the Kazakhstan border, hence their Near Eastern facial features *(detail, following page)*. They were purchased from an antiques dealer in Copenhagen who lives in an apartment over his shop, laden with private treasures: clients are allowed into this *sanctum sanctorum* on a limited basis to avoid the enormous disappointment when told the furnishings are not for sale. The sturdy Welsh dresser was purchased in London many years before for a house in the Caribbean.

ORIENTALISTS
TIMELESS LIVING
PAINTING

A large Guatemalan painting from the first half of the twentieth century has the unusual device of one figure lighting by a handheld flashlight another figure in the process of loading a donkey. A gooseneck lamp illuminates the painting, rather than a more conventional picture light, and also provides general lighting for the room. This console table is another example of late-eighteenth-century "Mexican Chippendale." The colonial translation of traditional English and other European forms resulting in bold exaggeration is particularly charming.

## DINING ROOM

The dining room is the most "modern appearing" room in this house, but still its furnishings span five centuries: two hard-edge painted shelves support a pair of Renaissance-style terra-cotta urns; a 1960s Lucite console table holds a bust of Apollo; a set of plastic and steel armchairs surround a Regency mahogany dining table; and a pair of late-fifteenth-century gilt pilasters in the form of classical nymphs (only one of which is shown) flank the window. A long, pleated silk ceiling light surmounts all of these elements. The mere listing of these pieces seems to suggest an unworkable mélange of periods and materials in a single room, but in fact they work charmingly well together in this traditional dining room overlooking a city green zone. It is a misconception that a contemporary space requires only stark modern furnishings; it is the arrangement and editing of the pieces that produce the desired modern aspect, and not the combination of periods. Modernism is really created by moderation in selection and usage.

The painted steel and glass shelves were ordered from an "accommodating" shop selling modern Italian glass displayed on similar stands. The shelves were not intended to be permanent features of the dining room, but merely to serve until "something better" came along. They were stocked with bottles of wine, absent of anything else to display in them. Today, the same shelves have been filled with a growing collection of blue-and-white Chinese export tureens and look very smart indeed. While the bottles of wine have been replaced, it is unlikely that the shelves will be replaced by "something better."

This table set for a dinner is decorated with Lalique crystal candleholders from the 1940s and strewn with porcelain mushrooms made for a window display several decades ago. These "mushrooms" were purchased at an interesting, small shop in Palm Beach, Florida, called Barzina, which is open for a few months during the "season," so as to allow its proprietor to travel around the world collecting unusual objects to restock the shop. While finding items on trips that can fit in a suitcase is a "gift to be relished," transport should never be an impediment to buying what one really wants. Vendors will gladly help arrange the shipping. A mahogany and gilt console table under an eighteenth-century Danish mirror holds a bar, set up for a small cocktail party. The gilded pilasters, of Florentine origin, that flank the dining room window (a detail shown here), were purchased in Venice, where, surprisingly, one can still find good and interestingly fine antique pieces.

A resin bust of Apollo seems to float in the air as it sits on a 1960s Lucite table. A set of nineteenth-century grisaille Creil plates depicting children at games are set for a salad course on top of ivy-patterned plates by Wedgwood, which are copies of the service made for Napoleon in 1815 during his captivity by the British at St. Helena.

A long steel and wood set of shelves along one wall of the dining area holds a large and beautiful Coalbrookdale dessert service that had been used for many years but was never otherwise displayed. Each plate is painted with a different flower. The long modern shelving has proved a perfect vehicle to show off all thirty-five pieces, giving them the aspect of a tame Damien Hirst; this same effect never would have been achieved were the plates to have sat demurely inside the best Regency breakfront.

## BEDROOM HALLWAY

At the end of the principal bedroom hallway, a set of four eighteenth-century German reverse paintings on glass depicting the biblical parable of the prodigal son grace the wall above an eighteenth-century Mexican Chippendale console table. The heavy frames, original to the paintings, had been painted black and orange, which made them hard to place and overwhelmed the delicate beauty of the paintings. After much hand–wringing, the frames were repainted in a dead white, which has improved their overall appearance immensely.

## MASTER BEDROOM

The four-poster bed was made for the room and has a tester that has deliberately been left uncurtained, and that simply defines the space in which the bed sits. Family photographs and children's crafts establish the master bedroom as the true hearth of the house. There is always a "tug" as to whether family photographs "belong" in reception rooms or should be relegated to private quarters. There is really no definitive answer to this, other than personal taste. The mirrors flanking the four-poster bed were custom-made for the room and are composed of five rectangular sheets of beveled mirror placed horizontally without a frame. Set behind the lamps on the bedside tables, they add light and sparkle to the room. On the walls, a Catherine Warren painting of a cypress tree, a set of shelves filled with photographs and a pair of eighteenth-century Chinese needlework tigers, and a round, framed fragment of eighteenth-century wallpaper found in Naples provide interest. On a low table, a large composite bowl holds new books waiting to be read. The nineteenth-century Swedish settee in front of the bed retains its original straw upholstery stuffing, which is surprisingly comfortable. None of these "antique" decorations detract from the basic modernity and simplicity of the room's decoration.

HISTORICAL ATLAS
ANCIENT ROME

The master bedroom has ample seating and provides its occupants with a private domain, not only for sleep, but also to read, work, and make merry with the children. The room looks out onto a shallow garden with ivy-clad walls. An eighteenth-century secretary of German origin is where all household accounts get settled. The master bedroom appears considerably less "decorated" than other rooms in the house. It is interesting to note that even in the most opulent of the late-nineteenth-century Newport mansion-styled "cottages," where gilt was spread as thick as jam in the reception rooms, most of the bedrooms were done simply and seemed more likely to be found in actual cottages than in the behemoths bearing the same name.

## DRESSING ROOM

An entire room of closets is a true luxury. This room had previously been a sizeable bedroom; however, because the house was built at a time when closets were very moderate in size, this space was converted into a dressing room for the master bedroom. A Tommi Parzinger cabinet has additional drawers for scarves and other small items of clothing. The Chinese rug of many, many colors was purchased at a local house sale. The 1950s upholstered armchairs are used more for discarded clothing than for sitting. The long mirror rests against a wall and the angle at which it is placed produces very flattering reflections.

## BOY'S BEDROOM

The often-held notions that children like bright and often jarring color combinations not favored by their parents and that they need to be housed in Tinkertoy-type rooms, are given the lie in this boy's bedroom, which is as attractive to the adult eye as it is the child's and gives full prominence to youthful collections of toys and books. A passion for soccer is expressed in the grisaille painting of French star Zinedine Zidane in a now-familiar position. The two-tier bedside tables are tea carts on wheels. Above the wall-mounted set of lacquered shelves are two framed featherwork pictures, a traditional Mexican handicraft; one depicts the Mexican eagle and the other, the American eagle. Both were found at a weekend antiques market in L'Isle sur la Sorgue. The standing lamp is screened with words reflective of an optician's chart.

O N
P A X
J O Y
S A V E
L O V E
P U R E

ON
PAX
JOY
SAVE

This bedroom has a small anteroom that has been converted into a studio with a large surface desk for homework or artwork. The tricolor Mexican flag over the small desk includes an image of the Virgin Mary as well as the initials "JC." It was made in the 1930s during the terrible "Cristo" wars in Mexico, when Christian practices were outlawed in many parts of the country. At that time, it was a capital offense to place religious images on the national flag, such as this one that was used by the Cristeros. The armchairs on either side of the desk are Italian and were made in the 1940s.

## BREAKFAST ROOM

The breakfast room's bold, horizontal-striped walls add width and interest to the narrow space *(preceding page)*. Various types of shelving provide storage for an ever-expanding collection of dishes. The dishes are set with an order that renders the utilitarian shelves attractive. Basically, the orderly placement of objects no matter how grand or insignificant can produce an aesthetically pleasing display. The set of early-nineteenth-century armchairs sits around a contemporary Italian glass and steel extension table. An immaculately garbed Spanish hussar in an early-nineteenth-century painting peers uneasily at the blue elephant in the contemporary painting on the opposite side. Despite being from very different periods, both are compatible as enhancements to the decoration. The room opens directly onto a terrace, where breakfast is had on fine days.

## KITCHEN

The kitchen is compact, functional, and pleasing to the eye. It suggests that in this house much attention is paid to the preparation of good meals. The Italian kitchen units were from a sample display in a stylish kitchen store; once purchased, they were reassembled to fit the house's existing kitchen space, requiring only the moving of the pantry door to allow sufficient wall space for the oven. The sink and stovetop unit was originally a freestanding "island": removing a countertop on one side allowed it to be placed intact against a wall. This wooden countertop was then cut in two and mounted as shelving on either side of the kitchen, providing additional storage space. The result was the acquisition of an excellent "kitchen" without the usual four-plus-month wait.

## PANTRY

The pantry holds the main collection of dishware and also houses twin refrigerators (not shown) that come in handy for a family that entertains regularly and often. A vertical bookcase was devised to hold a sizeable collection of cookbooks. A ladder on a rung that can be moved around the pantry was added to put the highest shelves within reach. Round baskets underneath offer a stylish and orderly means of storing wine and other beverages while conserving space.

a little taste of... china
a little taste of... italy
a little taste of... france
Pie
500 LOW-CARB RECIPES
fresco
BAKING with JULIA
THE NEW BEST RECIPE
FROM THE EDITORS OF COOK'S ILLUSTRATED
VEGETABLE
PASTAS
POLLO
FRANCESA
MEXICANA
GALLETAS
AL HORNO
POSTRES
PAPAS
SOPAS
PASTELES
VERDURAS
LAWSON
LAROUSSE
PARÍS
FLORENCIA
Sabores
TENTEMPIÉS
asiática
GRANDES RESTAURANTES

## TERRACE

A teak deck installed on the two levels between the main house and the guest cottage is furnished as an outdoor living room; a hanging candle chandelier enhances this "living room" aspect. Four maple trees planted into the decking provide shade and also help define the space. The upper deck, here set for a light breakfast, is directly outside and conveniently opens into the kitchen and breakfast room of the main house.

The deck is best enjoyed in the evening and at night, as the trees are still too young to provide complete shelter from the hot daytime sun. The "Venise" sign, probably from a restaurant, was found in London and adds a pleasant touch of whimsy to this outdoor "room."

## GUEST COTTAGE

This room in the cottage is furnished as a bedroom/sitting area to allow guests an opportunity to enjoy privacy during their visit. The headboard is covered in a burlap wonderfully painted with flowering vines and birds that was a gift from a superb Parisian decorator, Catherine Côle. The baskets hanging above the bed are Swiss artillery baskets, now filled with boughs. Above the sofa, a naive eighteenth-century copy of Raphael's *Persian Sybil*, found in a small town in Sweden during a Baltic cruise, graces the wall. On either side of it, the silver candleholders in the form of bows were acquired in Copenhagen. A pair of white-painted étagères was developed from Moholy-Nagy's original and holds a pair of miniature English-style secretaries complete with fall fronts, exterior drawers, and tiny interior drawers. A wirework chandelier—seemingly too large for the relatively small space—actually gives a sense of expansiveness to the room, as oversize pieces often do. It's better to do without a chandelier or hanging lamp if the ceiling is too low or the space seems too small to allow a reasonable-size fixture; a tiny ceiling light makes the space look even smaller, or the ceiling even lower.

When the house was purchased, the second room in the guest cottage had an inexplicable early-twentieth-century English flavor, probably due to a brick fireplace (not shown). This flavor dictated its current decoration, starting with an early-nineteenth-century painting of hounds by Samuel Spode hung over the bed. The headboard is upholstered in a 1950s-style fabric that oddly enough suggests Bloomsbury in the early twentieth century. The wall surrounding the mid-nineteenth-century lacquer–paneled-and-bamboo desk is covered with paintings, engravings, and other objects acquired over many years, in many countries. A wall such as this provides an opportunity to hang small impulse purchases that are not suitable for elsewhere and which need to be hung in orderly groupings that take into account size and color in order to have any prominence.

## GARDEN

The massive trunk of an old jacaranda tree together with luxuriant bamboo and ferns create a shady glen in the garden for an occasional midday meal.

# Country house

# A STATELY COUNTRY HOUSE

The phrase "house in the country" evokes multiple and similarly pleasurable images: a wooden dacha in Russia being reopened each year at the first sign of spring; a monumental and chilly "pile" in the gorgeous English countryside hoarding a noble ransom of Italian Renaissance paintings; incredible eighteenth-century furniture housed in a stone and slate-roofed château in France with grand and largely empty indoor spaces containing superb pieces of threadbare "Louis" furniture; or a Shingle-style cottage in New England, with lovely interior light and the sound of waves or wind in the pine forests. Whether formal or informal, a country house is not a place for serious activities other than tennis, golf, and horseback riding. What lies outside the house in the country is as important as or even more important than what is inside. And there should be many places, both indoors and outdoors, to perch and read a book or watch the changing weather.

The house shown here is considerably more formal than what is currently built as a country house, but nonetheless is enormously comfortable and affords any amount of opportunities for either privacy or companionship, as desired. The residents derive equal pleasure from the surprise of dressed-up evenings with formal table service as they do from cozy dinners in the kitchen.

The house was built only seven years ago but already has a weathered aspect that makes many first-time visitors assume it is decades or centuries older. Even the gardens have a precocious maturity. Possibly, the seeming age of the house derives from its construction, which was accomplished with no recourse to machinery except for a handheld saw used to cut the kitchen tiles that cover the deep door and window recesses. The core of the house is adobe (providing excellent insulation against summer heat and winter cold) covered with cement, then brick and then more cement and finally, on the exterior, rectangles of flat stone without surface mortar. The walls are almost one yard thick. All in all, the house was built by methods used over millennia. Although the plans were computerized, string and chalk-lines guided the builders.

This house is filled with furniture, fine art, and *objets d'art*, some inherited, some that have been used in other houses over a thirty-year period, and some that were purchased specifically for this house. As with any living situation, the decoration process is continuous and ongoing. The walls of the ground floor were originally painted in pinks, greens, yellow, and beige but have recently been repainted in a creamy white to reflect the interior calm of the residence that became more apparent after several years of its occupancy. Over the past seven years, furniture has been moved, added, and eliminated, demonstrating that the house is as organic as the gardens surrounding it. Despite the most elaborate planning and forethought, the realization of the true character of a house can be a gradual process and often needs to be respected by change.

Being a country house and not a primary residence, this house is used periodically, generally on weekends, and is always a joy to return to and sad to leave. New guests quickly adapt to its tranquility and the privacy that its diverse inner and outer spaces afford them. There are frequent house parties with four or five couples attending. Friday night supper is provided to late arriving guests. Saturday breakfast and dinner are offered as well as a Sunday brunch; with the rest of days given to tennis, golf, and other individual pursuits. Visitors usually become regulars.

## HOUSE EXTERIOR

The idea to cover the surface of the main house in unmortared cut local stone was suggested by a photograph of a house in Glasgow, Scotland *(preceding page)*. Originally, the exterior was to be finished in painted cement, but since the front façade is on an east-west axis facing south, it was thought that a light color would cause too much glare, and a dark color was never acceptable. It is remarkable that on rainy days the façade resembles so much the house in Scotland, as the porous stone becomes mottled when wet.

## ENTRANCE WAY

Upon passing through the entry gates, a series of surprises unfolds for the visitor, who has driven for several miles on a dirt country road bordered by dry, stark landscapes. The first is the sight of an apricot orchard and a lush green allée of ash trees along a cobblestoned lane. Then, a broad, well-tended lawn comes into view, with a row of dense arborvitae trees and the briefest glimpse of a large stone house of a yet-indefinable style. Only when the car enters the cobblestoned courtyard in front of the house can one see its full façade, which resembles an eighteenth-century château.

## FRONT HALL

Upon entering the front door, it is clear that this house is furnished formally, albeit with a sizeable dose of whimsy. A console table beneath a green and gilt trumeau mirror rests on two metal "horse" legs found in a local rummage shop; the legs were undoubtedly part of an equestrian statue, which makes one wonder where the rest of the piece now lies (or, indeed, how it stands). The table's wooden top was crafted and painted to resemble marble, rather than adding the weight of an equivalent piece of real stone. A nineteenth-century Della Robbia–style plaque hangs above the doorway to the living room. Watching it be raised to its present position was harrowing because of its weight and fragility.

The front hall leads directly into the living room, and from the front door one has a glimpse of the terrace behind. A marvelous faux-grained mid-eighteenth-century "William Kentish" corner cabinet found a "home" by being placed directly in the wall, as the house lacked any appropriate corner. Corner cabinets are hard to place in most houses and therefore tend to be considerably less expensive than "flat" cabinets of equivalent or even lesser quality. The cabinet contains a partial dessert service that was made in Paris by Dagoty for Marie Thérèse, the surviving daughter of Marie-Antoinette and Louis XVI who later became the Duchess of Angouléme; reputedly, it was later owned by Lord Byron, as is recorded on the back of one of the plates. The ceramic rondels on either side of the entry to the living room bear the profiles of male and female harvest gods and are nineteenth-century French majolica. Amusingly, the male of the pair bears a striking resemblance to the tennis player Boris Becker.

The walls of the front hall, like all the halls in the house, were painted to resemble stone by the most simple method possible: they were painted in a matte oyster white water-based paint, and then narrow horizontal and vertical white lines were added to suggest mortar. We first saw this faux-stone technique on the ground-floor walls of the Musée Nissim de Camondo in Paris. The figure of two seventeenth-century painted wood Chinese figures sharing a bowl of rice, which is supposed to bring luck, has hung on the walls of the owners' prior houses. The chandelier, in the shape of a Cardinal's hat, perhaps began its existence in the seventeenth century as a hat shop sign in Italy. The round table is Swedish and holds a bust of Ramses II along with a pair of metal Egyptian-figure lamps. An American-Indian maiden, one of the "four continents," stands on a windowsill; the other three "continents" remain to be discovered. The two large gilt bamboo-framed chinoiserie paintings that decorate the stairwell were inspired by a small pair of eighteenth-century engravings after François Boucher of children at play; two additional similar paintings (further up the stairwell, and not shown here) were extrapolated from the original pair.

## LIVING ROOM

This room is 30 feet long and 20 feet wide and has a rectangular windowed extension with doors that open onto a large stone terrace. It was deliberately "deformalized" by covering most of the furniture in the same beige-and-white striped chintz fabric. The grouping of furniture allows the room to work well both for large and small numbers of people. The room gains its determining architecture from eight fluted, wood columns that came from a ruined eighteenth-century hacienda. When first discovered, the columns were covered in ragged canvas that had been painted to resemble marble over a gesso base. Careful work revealed the fluted forms, which are periodically waxed to keep them from drying out. The columns were moved around the room in order to locate the most appropriate places for them. Once this was determined, cement bases were made on the chosen sites. Then, after the columns were affixed to their bases, cement capitals were created on top to connect them to the ceiling. This room, like several others in the house, has a set of portières on the door to the main hall which serve the purpose of keeping in heat, without the solidity of doors. Many of the objects and the furniture here came from prior residences; seeing items from different houses that one has lived in placed in a new setting often re-creates the initial pleasure of acquiring them, and adds greatly to the enjoyment of a new home. More than simply the aesthetic value of beautiful objects and paintings, these items arouse all the happy memories and stories of where and when each was found and acquired.

The pair of early-nineteenth-century bookcases flanking the sofa was found in Rome and holds, among other objects, two eighteenth-century English frames discovered in a basement storage room of a London antiques dealer. The mats of the frames are made of folded silver tinsel paper, simulating more costly crystals. These rare and exquisite objects remained empty for many years until an appropriate pair of German "dressed" figures on a painted paper landscape was found to fill them. The handsome large portrait on the wall portrays a nineteenth-century Turkish Janissary, whose hairless face indicates that he was a eunuch, hence his equivocal and expressionless face.

The dramatic painting above the fireplace of a bacchante girded in a leopard skin was purchased at an auction in Scotland; it was painted in the late nineteenth century by an American member of the British Royal Academy, Anna Lea Merritt. To one side of it, a bust of a vestal virgin, a resin copy of a marble original, rests on a two-tiered console table custom-made for the room (one of a pair), having

an apron of gilded Celtic knots. The engraving behind the bust, framed in the shape of a pylon with inlaid ancient Egyptian symbols—one of several in the house—is from the *Description de L'Egypte*, initiated by Napoleon. The wooden head is a detail of a pair of seventeenth-century German statues mounted on the walls flanking the doorway.

## TERRACE

The low-walled back terrace is set slightly above a broad gravel-filled expanse framed by a line of enormous juniper trees. Four 10-foot-long white wooden benches originally used at a railway station border three sides of its perimeter.

An old French silk washer is used as a planter for cacti; the wooden portion of the planter requires frequent applications of polyurethane to permit it to remain outdoors. The large cement planter on the terrace steps—one of a pair—was made for the house and resembles bamboo. A smaller planter with lion handles—also one of a pair—is made of colored metal and is a form that was common during the era of Napoleon III. An old zinc bathtub holds lavender grown from seed in the property's greenhouse.

Alfresco dining is attempted whenever the weather permits. Mild spring and fall evenings are seized upon for dinners outdoors, although warm throw rugs often need to be distributed at dessert time so that the meal can be finished outside.

The row of mature junipers framing the rear portion of the gravel terrace was among the few trees on the property when it was purchased. In front of the junipers, a cement fountain in the form of a horse trough set behind the house is capped by a headless bust of the Apollo Belvedere. The size of the juniper trees is manifested in relation to the long white bench.

## KITCHEN GARDEN

The kitchen garden, entered from a cobblestoned area outside of the kitchen and fenced in by arborvitae trees, has four large beds for herbs and some cutting flowers. Two pagoda-like structures were crafted from fallen tree limbs to hold climbing morning glory vines that provide shelter for plants needing refuge from full sunlight.

## DINING ROOM

The painted leaves on the ceiling above a silk-covered Tomas Borg hanging lamp are a device borrowed from Madeleine Castaing, who employed them on the ceiling of her dining room on Rue Bonaparte in Paris; there, over many cigarettes and champagne, I learned directly from the youthful nonagenarian the virtues of eclecticism and appreciation of the "lowly" as opposed to striving only for the "grand" in decorative schemes. The dining room has chairs of mixed origin: six are French with a nailhead trim and four are Swedish. Both are covered in the same fabric, which allows their easy relationship. For a large dinner party, white "ballroom" chairs with seat cushions in the same fabric as the other chairs are added. The two chests that stand at the end of the room are painted with scattered chinoiserie vignettes derived from a seventeenth-century German needlework screen. A pair of nineteenth-century metal aloe plants on the chests sharply punctuates the room's decoration.

Food, good conversation, friends, and family are the principal components of any dining room. The room's decoration should merely be a mood enhancer for the pleasurable experience of a dinner party. A beautifully set table is a gift to one's guests: the Venetian goblets with spiral blue and red stripes flecked with silver pick up the color of the service and salad plates.

A pair of tall armoires that date from the late Victorian era are coveted by most guests, who add their names to an unwritten list of willing purchasers in the unlikely event they are put up for sale. The portières at the doorway to the main hall are pulled closed before and after dinner parties—and sometimes during to retain warmth, if the night is cool. A pair of leaf-form vases, probably of French origin, was purchased in London and mysteriously took a year to arrive; never having seen their like before or since, the owners were delighted with the eventual arrival. The reverse paintings on glass are French in origin.

## LOWER HALL

Both floors of the house have long, east-west hallways with high, barrel-vaulted ceilings, which provide access to most of the rooms. These grand halls lend a sense of ceremony to the simple act of entering or leaving a room. The stone floor was laid when the house was built seven years ago, but being relatively soft and porous, it has already gained the appearance of considerable age. The Neo-classical lanterns were made for the house. All of the internal doors are paneled with mirrors to enhance their appearance. A long, late-nineteenth-century painting of hollyhocks frames one side of the hall and its surmounted picture fixture adds general light to the space.

COS·TERTIUM·FECIT
NAPARTE TOUCHANT LES PESTIFERES.

## DRAWING ROOM

The walls of this drawing room are adorned with multiple framed nineteenth-century Épinal cartoon lithographs depicting the career of Napoleon Bonaparte. Contemporaneous tile portraits of Louis XVI and Marie-Antoinette sit uneasily underneath the main grouping of the Napoleonic images. There are also several individual images of Napoleon's generals: pictured here is General Bertrand who followed the emperor to exile in St. Helena. The pair of silver-covered Napoleon III chairs (one is shown here, the other is across from the wooden table) in the room was originally made for the Indian market. The chairs are not identical in size: the larger one was made for a man, and the smaller for a woman.

Twin nineteenth-century étagères, made for use on a sailing ship, flank a daybed of the same era. The back legs of the étagères have brass disks with holes in the middle so they could be affixed to the ship's walls for stability. The charming lamps in the form of Asian musicians are made of terra-cotta. A colorful Turkish tribal rug from the mid-nineteenth century brings the room together—as a rug should. A detail of a mirrored wall urn, one of a pair in the room, was made by the late Frederick Victoria.

## LIBRARY

The library, like all corner rooms on the ground floor, has two windows and double French doors to the terrace outside. This sameness offers a pleasant repetition, while variations in the decoration of these four rooms provide visual stimulation. Aside from being very "unforgiving to any staining," a sisal rug can do wonders for a room's cohesiveness. The chimneypiece—like an identical one in the living room—was created while the house was in the last stages of its construction, when a group of stone columns intended for outdoor adornment were viewed as excessively decorative for their place on the house's rear façade. Cut down in size and joined with their cornice, they succeeded in "dressing up" what were originally intended to be bolection-type chimneypieces. The "stack of book" lamps were made for the house.

A pair of Catherine Warren paintings of torsos (only one of which is pictured) gives an electric surge to the otherwise calm decoration of the library. The plinths underneath were originally one square piece that was cut in half to make it more useful. From the large terra-cotta mask hovering over the front door to the busts placed in many of the rooms, it is clear that a major decorative theme in this house is the representation of the human face. Here, the faces of a nineteenth-century Oaxacan pitcher (astonishingly still intact after suffering two bullet holes during its existence) and an eighteenth-century English mannequin preside benignly over the room. The calligraphy plate was acquired many years ago from Katie Ridder's long-gone, but much lamented, decorative shop in Manhattan; she was as good at the selection of decorative pieces for a shop as she is a decorator, which is not surprising.

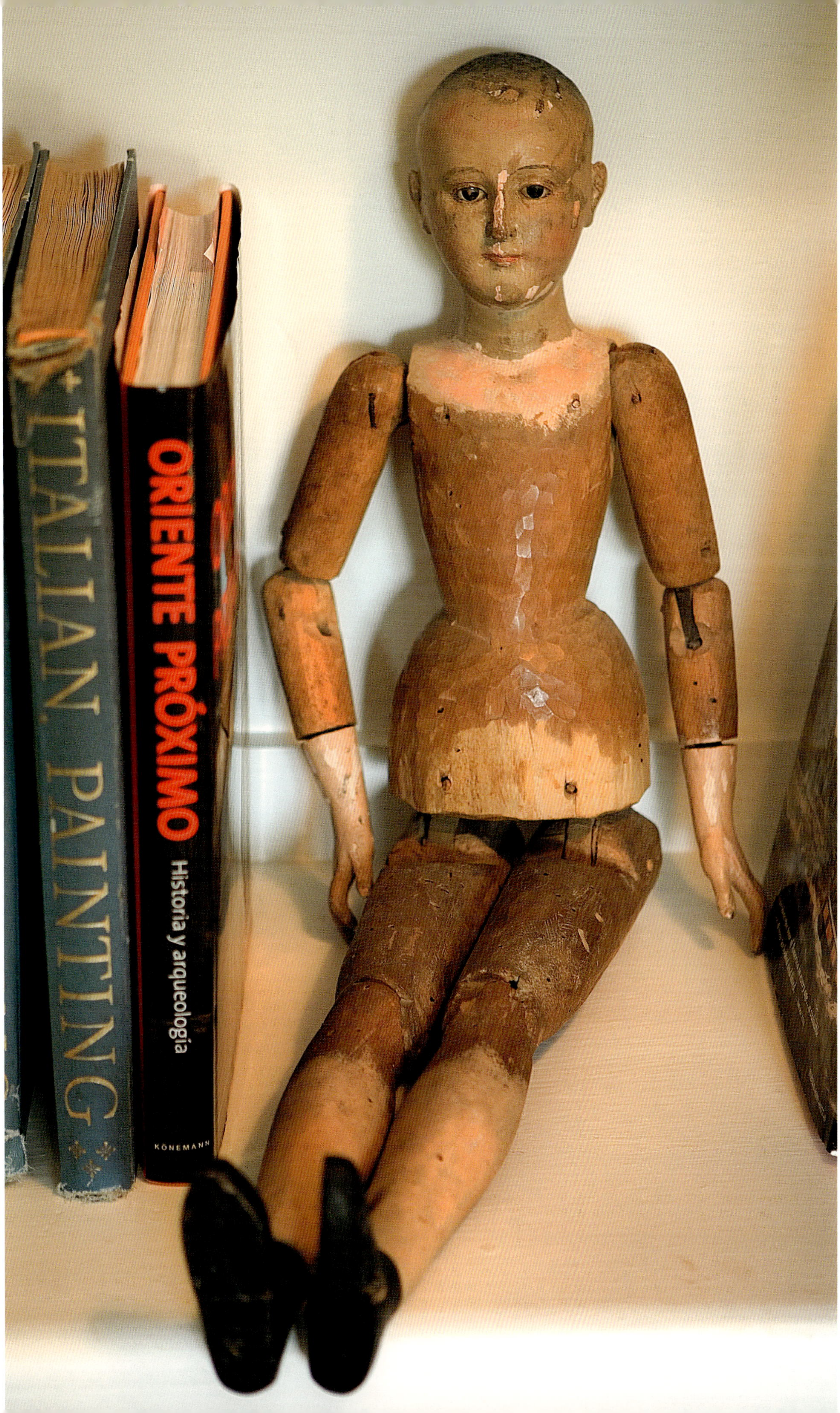
ITALIAN PAINTING
ORIENTE PRÓXIMO
Historia y arqueología
KÖNEMANN

## KITCHEN

The steel kitchen table provides both an effective workspace as well as a comfortable setting for family meals and informal dinners with friends. On the floor, a model of the Eiffel Tower announces the Francophilia of the owners; an engraving of the fall of the Bastille next to it is a reminder that the birthday of the lady of the house falls on the fourteenth of July, rather than being a sign of revolutionary persuasions.

The window over the stove looks out to a large and flourishing date palm, offering a pleasant view while cooking *(following page)*. A variety of baskets for both function and decoration are found throughout the house, and at least four large ones roost in the kitchen. Virtually every room has a basket full of blanket throws, useful for chilly winter nights.

S.PELLEGRINO

This large nineteenth-century cupboard was found in a small second-hand shop before the house plans had been completed. It remained in its many parts and was assembled only once the kitchen walls were in place. It fit perfectly between a doorway and a staircase hall—a remarkable achievement considering that despite computerized plans, all the spaces were defined and constructed from string lines and chalk marks on the ground. The cabinet's contents are arranged both decoratively as well as functionally, in the French tradition.

The kitchen counters are made of polished cement and lend a look of "age" in the house; they receive a waxing every three months to keep them water- and stain-resistant. The kitchen door shown here leads out to a parking area, to facilitate the bringing of groceries and other household necessities into the room. In the stairwell that leads to the bedroom hall, framed children's drawings and other charming items not really meant for display in the main rooms find a place.

DICK FRANCIS
DECIDER
The Last Word
A.N. WILSON
The Pebbled Shore
ELIZABETH LONGFORD
The SHEPHERD OF THE OCEAN
SAN FRANCISCO
Dolls' Houses in America
UNDUE INFLUENCE
DAVID MARGOLICK
PAPILLON

## STAIRCASE LANDING

The landing at the top of the main staircase has an early-nineteenth-century bookcase, now painted in a creamy white, which holds a selection of books that has recently been moved from the master bedroom. The curious blue-and-white marbleized cabinet, filled with Staffordshire figurines, probably began life as a stage prop; the upper cabinet has no back and had to be wired to the wall in order for it to stand upright. Two hand-colored engravings of oriental scenes by David Roberts flank the cabinet, and others appear in identical frames up and down the hallway. Beneath the engravings sits a pair of wooden Aesthetic movement side chairs.

## MASTER BEDROOM

The upholstered sleigh bed in the master bedroom is inviting: freshly laundered and ironed linen sheets, feather comforters, and a feather bed make the urge to climb into it irresistible. The walls and ceiling are covered in two different wallpapers; both, however, have a similar allover leaf pattern, one small and the other larger, in the same colors, which permits their harmonious coexistence. The charcoal drawing on a large canvas was a favorite object and finally found a home in an unexpected space between the beveled mirror screens. Between the screens is a long bench covered with books and magazines that was acquired from Madeleine Castaing. A cozy pink upholstered eighteenth-century Bergère-style chair sits in front of a pair of French doors; for additional seating, a pair of diminutive Herter chairs flanks a trefoil-form pouf. Among the room's decorative elements, the three Thornton engravings of botanicals are noteworthy for their remarkable straw frames, which were found at an antiques fair outside of Paris in a town called Chatoux, and a Staffordshire mask of a bacchante hung near the door is too pretty not to show in detail.

A gilded wooden medallion bearing the image of a young girl with a garland of painted leaves hangs on the wall above a Biedermeier desk in the Neo-Gothic style. While highly decorative, this a curious piece, as its main surface is too high to function as a desk, so it's only used to hold photographs and the contents of pockets at night. A Charles II fruitwood chest of drawers also holds, and is surmounted by, family photographs and portraits.

The corner fireplace was fashioned to resemble a Northern European tile stove. The multiple images of a jumping figure painted to order on commercial tiles are derived from Chinese-influenced seventeenth-century Mexican pottery. A small and fine Mogul painting of Western lovers, shown in detail, hangs in the center. In the master bathroom, hinges have been added to an old pair of the framed mirrors above the sinks, which serve as the medicine cabinet doors. All of the bathrooms in the house have the same decorative pattern, which provides stylistic continuity: black-and-white tile floors, white tile walls, and glass shower doors.

## LOGGIA

The loggia off the master bedroom, with its view of the tall juniper trees behind the house, provides a dose of adrenaline upon waking here in the morning. This space was originally open to the elements but, never being used for this reason, was subsequently closed by adding windows. It is now an inviting family meeting place for early-morning or late-night conversations.

## GIRL'S BEDROOM

Blue-and-white plaid and pink-and-white checks help prevent the sweetness of the floral wallpaper from becoming too "saccharine," while at the same time providing a joyous nest for a young girl. The upholstered bed in painted metal with metal ribbons climbing its posts surmounted by bouquets of flowers is pleasantly "over the top." A handsome bow-fronted George III chest of drawers keeps the room's decorative scheme from getting too out of control.

It is interesting to note that while some people can live easily in the midst of pattern and color variations, others most definitely cannot. In this house, however, multiple patterns are not a problem.

## BOY'S BEDROOM

Patterns of relatively muted browns and greens combined with nineteenth-century English furniture give a decidedly masculine cast to this teenage boy's room. The off-white walls were sponged in shades of brown to create vertical stripes. A nautical chest of drawers from the mid-Victorian period "quiets" the exotic.

The metal palm fronds on the bedposts, the early-twentieth-century hand-colored framed photographs of rural Egypt, the palms printed on the curtain fabric echoing the view outside, and the large elm wood secretary above a pale cotton zebra-patterned rug, create the exoticism of this bedroom.

## BOY'S BEDROOM

The basic furniture in this room—a Directoire meridienne and bed of the same period—is not what is generally considered appropriate for a child's room. However, one glance at the contents of the bookcases determines the age and interests of the youthful occupant. In a few years, by simply replacing the objects in the bookcases, the room can "mature as the child does," without necessitating major additional changes. This room also features a mid-Victorian nautical chest of drawers; nautical pieces have a decidedly masculine cast and are excellent pieces for boy's rooms. An amusing and naïve copy of a Landseer painting hangs above the bed.

America A Patriotic Primer
RE-ZOOM
Dr. Seuss
Gillian Wolfe
Adventures in Art
Golden Book
Chicago 2001–2002
Cat and Beaky Boo
Big Lift-and-Look Book
MERMAID AND OTHER FAIRY TALES
FIRST MOTHER GOOSE
WALKER BOOKS

Aggressive layering of sophisticated colors, fabrics, and objects creates a visual exuberance entirely appropriate for a young child. The kneehole desk painted in a colorful faux leopard-type scrim was made for the room. An eighteenth-century engraved portrait of a young boy was purchased because it bore so striking a resemblance to the room's occupant. The frame was painted as a copy of a very playful Venetian piece that is of the same period as the engraving.

## GUEST BEDROOM

The headboard of the bed in this room is a deeply beveled mirror, which most likely was previously used over a sideboard in a dining room; it is 62 inches long and fits a queen-size bed. It is extraordinary how blue and white can sharpen and add vitality to any grouping of colors, and what could be more "blue and white" than the fresh chinoiserie-painted images on the chests of drawers made for this room? The fall-front desk was made in Portuguese Goa during the late eighteenth century and has bone and ebony inlaid details.

A grained, English highboy, a pair of Napoleon III plant stands, a Goan ivory-and-ebony inlaid secretary, an American Impressionist painting, and a corner fireplace tiled with traditional Mexican colonial images in blue and white, all meld easily with a backdrop of English wallpaper and French fabric. The beautiful curtains in this room, along with those in the rest of the house—were made under the direction of Glenn Lavinder of Greensboro, North Carolina. The heavily-tufted Victorian armchairs were purchased in London and the original tufting was recreated in the principal fabric used in this room.

## GUEST HOUSE

The broad, sweeping cobblestone courtyard in front of the main house is bordered on three sides by ash trees and on one side by a guest/service building in half-timber style. This was done to reflect the structures at the Hameau de la Reine in Versailles, France, and also to suggest that its construction predated that of the main house. The doors and the windows on the ground level were made to resemble a stable. Reliable Virginia creeper has begun to cover much of the building.

Glorious morning glory vines have enveloped the posts of the awning around the main door. Firewood stacked outside is obtained from the pruning of the trees on the property or the occasional loss of a tree from natural causes. The quaint cement hounds positioned on the low terrace wall were made locally, in the spirit of a pack seen on top of a gate to a château in France.

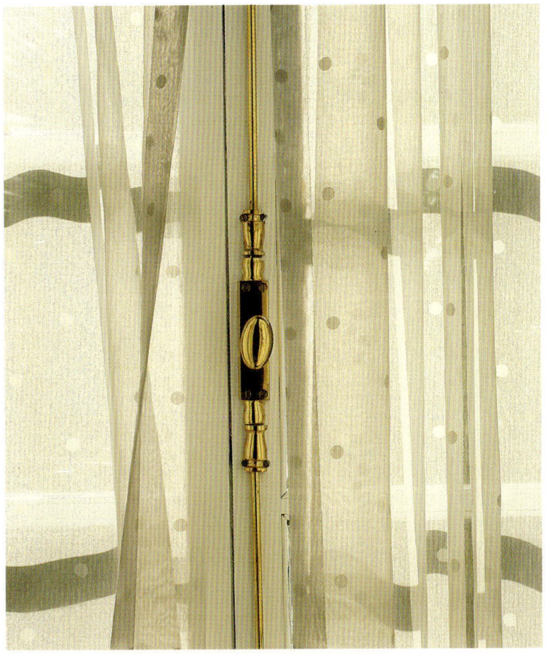

## GUEST HOUSE SUITE

Located on the second floor of the guest house, this somewhat Alpine bedroom/sitting room suite is filled with light from its six windows. Separated from the main house, the space allows a guest privacy, which is especially appreciated on a lengthy visit. It is furnished more as a bedroom in a summer house, as indeed it is used only during the warmer months.

## EXTERIORS AND SWIMMING POOL

Walking across the broad avenue of pea gravel bordered by tall, conical trees, one can easily be transported to the gardens of Ninfa in Italy or Chaumont in France. No part of this garden is a deliberate copy of somewhere else in the "Las Vegas" sense; rather it evokes the spirit of other places where one has been. The unusual cement plinths in the form of tree trunks were fabricated locally. The serene terra-cotta mask above the front door of the house came from Argentina. The swimming pool is surrounded by the ubiquitous arborvitae *(following page)*. Given the extremes of temperature, these trees are the most reliable for surviving winter's frosts.

When this property was purchased, it was largely a desert but for a long, east-west line of very tall junipers at one end and another of mature mulberry trees in the middle. Not surprisingly, these elements sparked the interest of the land, and today they remain important components of the landscape, notwithstanding the planting of several hundred other trees that are now maturing, as well as thousands of new plants.

The palms in front of the house were about 6 feet tall when they were planted in the soil seven years ago; today, the fronds will soon rise above the roofline. Ferns grow exuberantly from spring through the fall, but need to be placed inside the greenhouse in order to survive the winter. The painted wrought-iron lanterns on the outside walls were made for the house.

## GARDENS

As the owners wanted to experiment with plants not typically grown in the area, the gardens were designed very much on a trial-and-error basis, without a real knowledge of what would survive in the harsh fluctuations of the winter temperatures (which vary from 25 degrees Fahrenheit at night to 75 degrees at midday). Cuttings and seeds were brought back from travels abroad in the hopes that English lavender, Italian basil, Roman pine, and European boxwood (which is the principal component in the scent of most European gardens) might survive. So far, the results have been mixed, but there have been some notable successes.

A secret garden was begun seven years ago with the planting of 1-foot-high Texas privet plants; they have since grown to provide 5-foot-high walls.

The variety of the property's leaves, flowers, and trees are interesting both as a panorama and viewed close-up. Here, the twisted trunks of the mulberry tree, which is a soft wood that responds to the winds, appears like a dancing couple or a strutting pair of legs.

Billowing rosemary and Russian sage hedges, which are shown here, appear all over the property, and new plants are grown from seeds or cuttings in the greenhouse, along with lavender and boxwood, as well as tender French and Italian lettuces, basil, and tomatoes intended for the kitchen.

## PERGOLA

A cross-shaped pergola was built from fallen tree branches collected in the vicinity of the house, and some eight years ago more than one hundred small white climbing rose bushes were planted against the structure's upright supports. Today, the climbing roses on the pergola produce thousands of flowers in their first bloom and the wonderful scent is borne across the property by the spring breezes. As shown in the detail, their own branches are probably substantial enough to hold the entire structure. Several of the plants turned out to yield pink roses, and their slight rosy intrusion among the overall whiteness is very pleasing. There are four large beds on each of the four angles of the pergola, which are planted in abundant and multicolored zinnias in the spring and summer, and then in rye or another winter wheat in the fall and winter. The zinnias provide endless flowers for the house and friends for five months, and the winter wheat gives some vegetal forms to look at when no flowers will grow.

## ALLÉES

The benches and plinths that line the gravel walk under the allée of mulberry trees were made locally of cement mixed with feathers to lighten their weight. The large round pots, seemingly terra-cotta, are also made of cement—but without feathers—and thus most probably will never be moved from their sites. In the spring, the ripe mulberries that fall to the ground from the trees stain the pea gravel path a pleasing purple.

## TOWER

The irrigation system on this part of the property required a large cistern that reaches 5 feet above ground. A tower was built to cover it and act as a "folly;" at the same time, it provides additional storage space for garden equipment.

In the evening, the stillness and darkness of the countryside are broken only by soft lights and voices emanating from the house *(following page)*. There is no outdoor lighting to enhance—or rather, spoil—the beauty of the night, other than the moon and the stars. Gas-lit lanterns are supplied to guests desiring a walk in the gardens after dark; they also assure the eight dogs that reside on the property that the walker is a friend welcomed by their masters, and not a foe.

# Lakeside house

## A LAKESIDE WEEKEND RETREAT

A house by a lake (or on any water's edge) is a delicious treat. Not only does proximity to water allow the observer to marvel at the changing moods of the sky but also the changing moods of the water. More than any other type of house, a house by the water gives full meaning to the wonderful Italian expression *dolce far niente*, or "sweetness is doing nothing." Even a house in the country beckons those so inclined to prune trees and work in the garden but a house by the water allows one to avoid any such exertions and concentrate on boating, sailing, or swimming—or just watching the currents and kaleidoscopic colors of the water. This house is situated by a very large artificial lake and is built on the upper remnants of what once were mountains surrounding the now-inundated valley. This factor, together with the general scarcity of land around the lake, explains why the house is built on five levels, with the top level having a swimming pool, an outdoor kitchen, and outdoor dining and living rooms. All of the rooms face south and have spectacular views of the lake and the pine-tree-covered tops of the "former mountains" where clouds are often trapped. Every room also has access to a terrace or balcony. The house is furnished eclectically and casually in a predominantly modern persuasion, although never compromising on comfort.

The house was totally rebuilt from an older construction that took little advantage of its remarkable site and left the brilliant, clear light to be enjoyed only from the outside. This has been changed, and now the light is dramatically brought into all the rooms providing the sensation that on moving indoors the lake and all its brilliance accompany one inside. The fifth floor where the pool is located is entirely new and its construction was truly a feat of engineering. Aside from the fact that all of the building materials had to be carried up steep and precarious scaffolds from the ground level, the pool is cantilevered over what is now the bedroom hall. In the style of the region in which the house is located, all halls and rooms other than the kitchen have pine beam ceilings that retain their marvelous fragrance. The scent of pine is enhanced by the use of resin-filled pine sticks to start fires in the fireplaces. All balconies and terraces have pots of tall laurel trees to add green to the views of lake and sky. In addition, the main terrace of the house, which is located on the third level of the house, has a small, well-tended lawn, and borders of mature gardenia plants. A garden on the sixth level is being developed on a trial-and-error basis with grass and white Japanese irises.

Although there are five bedrooms, the family generally comes to this house alone to enjoy selfishly the enormous peacefulness that the house provides and to unwind from mid-week duties. However, they lend the house to friends so that they can enjoy the same pleasures by themselves.

## EXTERIORS

The lake is the raison d'être of Valle de Bravo, a weekend resort town two hours from Mexico City, with its calm and quiet mornings and afternoons filled with sailboats, spinnakers, regattas, motorboats, tourist launches, windsurfers, kayaks, canoes, and noisy Jet Skis. All celebrate the beautiful, sometimes green, sometimes blue, often steel-gray waters. Therefore, the style and decoration of any home is second to the presence of the lake. While of course a house here needs to be comfortable and appealing to the eye, it should never interfere with the primary purpose of providing a place to live by the lake.

## ENTRANCE AND STAIRCASES

This house is built on five levels—six, if one includes the garden above the top pool level. Not surprisingly, the various staircases form a vital element in the design of the house. They need to meet their purpose and be attractive, without calling undue attention to themselves.

## TERRACE

The main floor of the house, which includes the indoor living room, dining room, and kitchen, as well as one guest bedroom, is actually three stories above ground level and has a neat and well-maintained small green lawn in front of the principal rooms.

A shallow outdoor fireplace supplies an unexpectedly large amount of warmth in the frequently chilly winter nights. This terrace is used primarily in late afternoons and evenings. Seating areas are created with armchairs grouped around two large, low tables, one being 9 feet long. They provide a comfortable spot to take informal meals, or to play board and card games. The terrace overlooks the lake but also a paddle tennis court (not shown) and the sound of rackets hitting balls adds to the agreeable ambience of the space.

## LIVING ROOM

Since the preference is to be outdoors if weather permits, the indoor living room is rarely used. Even so, the room has to provide an appealing place to sit when cold or rainy nights force everyone inside. The pair of leather and chrome armchairs was purchased from a relatively new shop in Mexico City called Urbana, which carries extensive lines of first quality Spanish, French, and other European furniture, all bringing a clean, modern approach to traditional forms. The existence of this shop made the furnishing of this house relatively easy since fewer pieces had to be made or imported. The black-painted octagonal tables with silver fittings are Moroccan and have some age. The long, triangular wall lights were found in West Palm Beach at the shop of John and Nanci Wilson, which specializes in unusual and large pieces of twentieth-century origin and earlier, to be used in ways that weren't originally intended. The square cocktail table came from Lars Bolander, whose shops can always be counted on to provide beautiful as well as aesthetically-pleasing functional pieces, both old and new.

ENGLISH HOUSE
MESA MEXICANA
ISLAMIC ART and ARCHITECTURE

This room is fitted with a great number of pairs, which suits the symmetric bias of the owners: black and silver-fitted Moroccan tables; lead-framed square mirrors; red lacquer Chinese stools in front of the fireplace; lead collages by Louise Nevelson; and the list goes on. The cast-iron wall lights—one with the face of Poseidon, and the other that of a water nymph—were originally decorations on a nineteenth-century pier in Brighton, England, that was destroyed long ago. They were acquired in London twenty years ago and have been moved from one house to another over the years, sometimes being used indoors, and at other times, outdoors.

## DINING ROOM

The dining room has a monastic quality that disappears the moment the table is set and a lively meal is in progress. The unusual driftwood chandelier serves not so much for light as to set the mood in the same manner as the candles. The metal lamp of bearers is also more for effect than illumination.

The table settings are generally kept as simple as the room furnishings, but are always interesting in the combination of dishes, glasses, and flowers. The large framed charcoal drawing that hangs above the bombé-fronted commode is by Henri Regnault and was presumably done as a preparatory work for a painting. It portrays a particularly gory and violent battle scene, which fortunately in the evening is muted thanks to its charcoal medium and the dim lighting.

## KITCHEN

The stove is a commercial unit, with two ovens, six burners, and a grill. Its industrial appearance and that of the exhaust above complete the sleekness of the kitchen design. The kitchen has a window that opens onto the indoor dining room; it is kept open during the day for the light and view of the lake, and closed with a wooden shutter at night when the dining room is in use.

## PANTRY

All of the cabinets shown were made for the kitchen and were painted in the same pale beige color. The pantry leads to the service stairs, which in turn ascend to the pool level. A plant stand holds a variety of potted fresh herbs for the kitchen.

## MASTER BEDROOM

The master bedroom enjoys an exceptionally high ceiling and has an attic story that is used as an office, which opens onto the bedroom through high windows in the wall in back of the bed. It is accessible only by a staircase from the master bedroom. Among the decorative objects are three high-fashion photographs by Deborah Turbeville.

A mixture of periods and styles is employed throughout this relatively spare and contemporary house in order to give it distinction. A Barbados-style bed was designed for the space. The Lucite bookshelves were originally made for the owner's mother in the 1970s. A green-lacquer Chinese desk is flanked by a painted Swedish chair and a Victorian upholstered armchair.

The contemporary aspect of the bedroom, like that of the other rooms, is created by moderation in the use of furniture and objects, rather than by employing "modern" furniture exclusively. It's the editing of what's used, rather than the periods of the pieces used, that creates acceptable and comfortable "modernity."

A charming glazed pottery dog from the 1930s—oddly attributed to Hermès—stands upon an Edwardian-era straw and bamboo chest of drawers. The stairs lead to the attic office. Here, as in most rooms in the house, the master bath boasts a splendid lake view. The only color other than white used in this bathroom, as is the case with every other bathroom in the house, is a blue-black polished granite on the counters.

## BEDROOM HALLWAY

The long and wide bedroom hallway also serves as a library. The three bookcases were constructed to house oversize art books in the bottom tall cubicles, magazines in the two higher ones, and regular books in the top shelves. The decorative pair of legs on a stand was undoubtedly part of a statue of a saint; the blue underclothes are a giveaway of their "saintly" provenance.

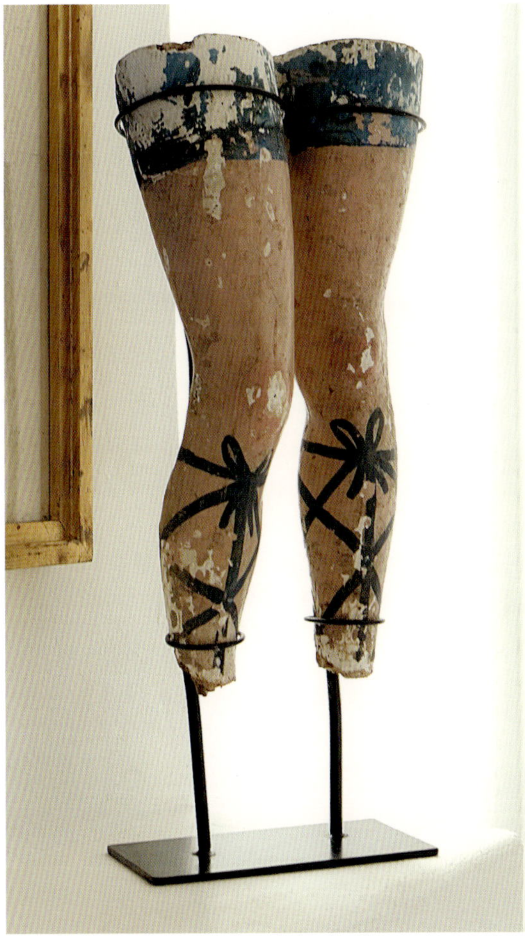

## GUEST ROOM

The large Barbados-style bed was built for this room, as were the vertically striped bedside chests of drawers. The elaborate tin mirrors are an example of Mexican folk art at its best, and mirrored lamps reflect the room's patterns. A nineteenth-century Chinese desk serves as a dressing table; a modern Orientalist painting hangs above it. The bathroom en suite with this bedroom is long and ends with a window overlooking the lake, which resembles a framed painting. The part of the room where the window is situated has a large glass skylight so that the entire area bursts with light.

Hadrian's Villa and Its Legacy

ZOOL
HAVE
150 Years of
Photo Journalism

## CHILD'S ROOM

The sofa, designed for this space, doubles as a bed for guests of the boy who occupies this room. The walls are hung with three playful vintage posters of the Copenhagen Zoo, and a large oil painting by Andriacci, a contemporary artist from the Oaxacan School in Mexico.

As with all of this house's rooms, this one has a balcony with a wonderful view. A telescope permits one to see who is coming and going on the lake, or to gaze at the moon and stars at night. A metal "ladder" acts as a drying rack for often-used bathing suits. The desk was made to fit into a niche in the wall and has multiple cubbyholes and shelves for an accumulation of books and other objects. The bath lacks a view but boasts a large skylight, and its private areas are concealed behind frosted glass.

## GUEST ROOM

Another guest room with a view of the lake has a low ceiling but, like the other rooms, has the same oiled wood beams so characteristic of Valle de Bravo. Adding a splash of color, the orange fabric on the chaise longue depicts Moro Castle in Havana and was found in Stockholm. The woven bed was made locally for the room.

¡HOLA!

¡HOLA!
SOLO

## GUEST ROOM SUITE

The spacious sofa in the sitting room doubles as a king-size bed, and an additional queen-size bed behind the louvered screen accommodates any overflow of young visitors or a family with young children. The paintings are early-twentieth-century renderings of two different steps in the pulque-making process: pulque, a mildly alcoholic beverage, dates back to the pre-Columbian era in Mexico and continues to be used today to warm young children and adults in the cold early mornings in the country.

## OUTDOOR DINING ROOM, KITCHEN, AND POOL

In addition to the blue-tiled pool, the fifth story, which commands the most majestic and panoramic view of the lake, has an outdoor living room, dining room, and kitchen. These areas are used mostly during the day and for dinner on warm nights. At night, the lake and the landscape on the far shore disappear into the pitch-black darkness, broken only by a few house lights and the occasional tourist party boat that cuts across the lake blaring popular music as it moves quickly into the night. The furnishings of the fifth level are even sparer than those of the lower levels, and the space is completely bare of decorative objects, as the view of the lake and mountain scenery would overwhelm any attempted decorative competition. However, the long black-tinted dining table and surrounding black-and-tan bistro chairs are certainly very stylish yet functional objects. The kitchen is separated from the dining room area by a long narrow white-painted cement counter that has open and closed cupboards on its side facing the kitchen equipment, and is used for storage of dishes and other paraphernalia related to cooking. A tall French bottle drying rack sits on the counter and holds assorted drinking glasses and coffee cups.

## OUTDOOR LIVING ROOM

The outdoor living area has a casual pair of long sofas and two armless wicker chairs. The sofas and their multiple pillows are covered in Pierre Frey Indoor/Outdoor fabric that has survived four years of sheltered but exposed space remarkably well; its colors remain fresh and vibrant. A large painted wrought-iron chandelier made to resemble coral has also withstood the weather well.

## ACKNOWLEDGMENTS

We thank Michel Zabé and his assistant Enrique Macias for capturing the spirit as well as the beauty of the properties depicted in this book. Thanks are due to Carmen Cordera Lascurain for her vision and perseverance, and to Emilio Breton for his unflagging professionalism; and we are grateful to both of them for their attention to detail and design. We also want to thank our editor, Sandy Gilbert, whose gentle prodding at all hours of the day and night pushed us to achieve a product beyond our original expectations. Our friends, Veronica Lacayo de Gomez and Christine Bell, are thanked here for their constant encouragement and enthusiasm. Last, but not at all least, we thank Marco Ausenda and Charles Miers for publishing our book.

Design: Carmen Cordera Lascurain: carmen@drafftdesign.net / Emilio Breton: emiliobreton@mac.com